WRITING

BASIC
WRITING
SKILLS

Peter W. Preksto Jr.
and
Patricia S. Schaefer

Creative Education, Inc.
Mankato, Minnesota

Library of Congress Cataloging in Publication Data

Preksto, Peter W.
  Writing.
  (Basic Skills Library)

  SUMMARY: Introduces basic English grammar and
presents exercises for developing writing skills.
    1. English language—Composition and exercises. [1. English
language—Composition and exercises]   I. Shaefer,
Patricia S., joint author.   II. Title.   III. Series.
PE1413.P7   808'.042   79-15800
ISBN 0-87191-716-5

Table of Contents

Introduction

Talking is managed with the help of scowls and other facial expressions, sweeping arms and other physical gestures, and shouts and other oral inflections. People who speak English have mainly agreed on how to emphasize some words to help make their meaning clear. For example, we generally understand that a sarcastic tone of voice can entirely change the meaning of an ordinary sentence. Think of the two meanings of: "John is *certainly* a good dancer." Depending on the tone of voice used, we would respond either by agreeing that John *is* indeed a good dancer, or else by laughing at his two left feet on the dance floor.

Writing is a completely different matter. When you write, your face is behind a blank mask, your hands are tied, and your lips are sealed. Written communication must be the result of skillful handling of the naked words. A good writer can take those bare words and turn them into a brilliant flash of colorful meaning. Such a writer can express any emotion, explain any idea, and describe any scene so that it is as clear and sharp as if we actually saw it with our real eyes.

Everyone will have the occasion to write something which should make perfect sense. There are times when a person needs to write a letter of apology for some embarrassing moment, or when a parent must explain a child's behavior in a letter to a teacher, or when a reader wishes to compose a letter to the editor of a newspaper. Being misunderstood can be serious business in these cases. To avoid that problem, every writer of any kind has the responsibility to learn something about this difficult craft. The rules of good writing are the same for every kind of writing—from advertising to poetry.

This book will help you in several ways to learn or to remember how to write. First, there is a review of grammar, the bare bones of the spoken and written language.

There is a brief review of some basic rules of punctuation. Punctuation doesn't always seem to be essential to successful, clear writing, yet entire meanings can be lost with one misplaced comma. You must learn to use correct punctuation consistently, too, or your readers will lose confidence in your message.

The next section is a list of basic writing rules. These rules aren't about what kind of paper you should type on or how to sit at your desk. They are lessons to help you make yourself understood and to keep your reader awake.

The last part of the book contains writing exercises so that you can practice what you have learned. You will find that the more you practice your writing, the easier and better it will be.

The Parts of Speech

All words can be placed in eight categories called the parts of speech. The parts are nouns, adjectives, pronouns, verbs, adverbs, prepositions, conjunctions, and interjections.

After writing a sentence or a paragraph, you should examine it to see if its grammar is reasonable. Is it loaded with adjectives? Have you used the correct cases for your pronouns? To be able to answer these and other questions, you must be familiar with the parts of speech.

The parts of speech can be identified by looking at your sentence and asking a series of questions about it. Is there a naming word? What is the action? Is there a linking word? The answers to these questions will help you identify the parts of speech. These parts of speech are all very different from each other and are easy to learn.

Here are the questions to ask and what the answers to those questions mean. A definition of the part of speech and some examples accompany each question.

NOUN

Is there a naming word?

A **noun** is the name of a person, place, idea, or thing.

The *candle* burns slowly.
George Washington is the father of our country.
Justice is blind.
An *aquarium* may contain many fish.
The *jury* has reached a decision.

ADJECTIVE

What kind of? Whose? How many?

An **adjective** is a word that modifies a noun or a pronoun. Words that sit in front of a noun or pronoun and serve as a noun marker are called articles. Some of them are: *the, a, an.*

The organ played *a merry* tune.
He gazed off into *the wild blue* yonder.
My cat finally had kittens.
This cap belongs to *an old* fisherman.
Neither one is correct.
Our clock has only *one* hand.
This is *the first* time I noticed.

PRONOUN

Is there a word that takes the place of a naming word?

A **pronoun** is a word that takes the place of a noun.

He threw the ball through the window.
Those are my mittens.
The tickets are given to *anyone*.
John, *who* will be going with us, is late.
I am going by *myself*.
You yourself can own this great car.
Be polite to *one another*.

VERB

What is the action?

A **verb** is a word that indicates action or a state of being.

Sheila *ate* the lunch.
The audience *talked* loudly.
It *is* I who called. (See a note on this type of
verb at the end of this section.)
   Verbs can also be changed into a form called
"verbals." (See a note on them at the
end of this section.)

ADVERB

What kind of action? Where? How? When?

An **adverb** is a word that modifies a verb, an adjective, or another adverb.

It snowed *today*.
I set the package *down*.
The milk froze *quickly*.
She made a *wonderfully* decorated cake.
The room was *fairly* quiet.

PREPOSITION

Is there a word that places one word in relation to another?

A **preposition** expresses the relation of a noun or a pronoun to some other word in the sentence.

Send the letter *to* Maria.
Between you and me, I hear there's trouble brewing. (See note on this type of preposition at the end of this section.)
Below the bridge, but *above* the stream, John swung *by* a rope.
The kettle is *next* to the pot.

CONJUNCTIONS

Is there a linking word?

A **conjunction** connects words, phrases, or independent clauses.

The sun was bright, *and* my eyes were closed.
You may go *but* must return early.
Either give me some candy, *or* I'll scream.
The sky turned green, *which* made me uneasy.
I know that it's true *because* I was there.
Ann dropped an egg into her stereo; *therefore* it wouldn't work.

INTERJECTION

Is there a word that exclaims or expresses surprise?

An **interjection** is an exclamatory word that expresses strong or sudden feeling. It has no other grammatical function in the sentence.

Oh! a spider.
She cried, "*Alas,* my lunch fell in the sewer."
Bah, humbug!

Notes

1. VERBS   Words which link a subject with a predicate noun or adjective are called copulative or linking verbs. It is useful to be familiar with the linking verbs because a predicative noun following one always takes the nominative case. Examples: It *is* I. We are *they* who called. It was he *who* dropped the pitcher. It would *seem* he didn't really want to go.

These are the linking verbs: be, am, is, are, was, were, being (and all other forms of the verb *to be*), seem, appear, look, sound, feel, continue, remain, taste, smell, become, grow, stay.

2. VERBALS   Verbals are verb forms which act as nouns or adjectives. There are three kinds of verbals.

Gerunds: A verb used as a noun. Example: *Walking* is fun.
Participle: A verb used as an adjective. Example: The *playing* children ran into the street.
Infinitive: A verb used as a noun, usually introduced by "to." Example: The car was unable *to stop.*

3. PREPOSITIONS   A noun or pronoun governed by a preposition is always in the objective case. For example, "Give the ball to *me*," "Phoebe and I are flying with *him*." You cannot say, "Give the ball to *I*." This sounds awkward, and it doesn't mean what you intend.

The Parts of the Sentence

Every sentence is made up of several parts: the action, the person or object talked about, the person or object receiving the action, and more. You will learn that certain parts of the sentence are weaker than others and should be avoided in good writing.

As with the parts of speech, you can identify the parts of a sentence by asking questions about it. The answers will help you find out what part you have located. Examples of the parts of the sentence are shown with the questions.

PREDICATE

1. What is the action or state-of-being word?

The dog *bit* my leg.
He *was* an excellent pet.

SUBJECT

2. Who or what is it that . . . ?

Carson loaded the rifle.
The crowd waved their hands.

DIRECT OBJECT

3. Acts on whom or what?

Ruth heaved *the sack* over the fence.
I pushed *the car* out of the garage.

INDIRECT OBJECT

4. To or for whom? To or for what?

She hit the ball directly to *him*.
I gave *Mary* my gum.

ADVERBIAL COMPLEMENT
place

5. (a) Where?

I hiked with Andy *to the park*.
With an escaped convict in his car,
the man drove *west*.

ADVERBIAL COMPLEMENT
cause

5. (b) Why?

He threw out the soup *because it was watery*.
They raised money *from selling pop at the stand*.

ADVERBIAL COMPLEMENT
time

5. (c) When?

Yesterday I couldn't start the car.
School opens *in the fall*.

ADVERBIAL COMPLEMENT
manner

5. (d) How?

Looking *around suspiciously*, Mary whispered a secret to her friend.
The hobo sauntered along *whistling a happy tune*.

ADVERBIAL COMPLEMENT
purpose

5. (e) What for?

He turned the key to *unlock the door*.
Hoping for a reservation, she called the hotel.

ADVERBIAL COMPLEMENT
possessive, material

5. (f) Of whom? Of what?

The cloth *of silk* sold most quickly.
The sword *of the prince* was said to be magic.

ADVERBIAL COMPLEMENT
source

5. (g) From what? From where?

The ship came *from the island of Crete.*
I began to sneeze *from the dust.*

ADVERBIAL COMPLEMENT
agent

5. (h) By whom? By what?

The car was driven *by a young man.*
Our home was designed *by an architect.*

ADVERBIAL COMPLEMENT
instrument

5. (i) By means of what?

We went *by trolley* to the fair.
She sliced the bread *with a sharp knife.*

ATTRIBUTIVE

6. Which? What kind of?

He chose the *smallest* chocolate.
Peter Sellers, *the famous comedian*, had a heart
   attack.

Special Aids

1. Conjugation

A verb has several voices, moods, tenses, numbers, persons, and forms. When they are all written down they make an impressive list. A chart showing the verb in all its glory is called a conjugation.

Some verbs, such as *play*, *call*, *talk*, and *walk*, keep their same basic form throughout the entire conjugation. We say, "I *walk*. He *walks.*" However, other verbs change to an entirely different word when used in different ways. Verbs which stay the same are called *regular* verbs. Verbs which change through the conjugation are called *irregular* verbs. *Is*, *run*, *eat*, *do*, and *have* are irregular verbs. We say, "I *run* every day. I *ran* last week. He *is* in town. He *was* far too late. Can you *do* this puzzle? I've *done* it badly."

Knowing the conjugation of verbs can help keep your writing clear and strong. For example, writing in active voice is much more effective than writing in passive voice. Remembering the difference can help you toughen your writing. It is also easy to change moods within a single paragraph, especially when writing a summary. A conjugation shows you how to stay in the same voice, tense, person, and mood.

Conjugation Terms

These are definitions of the terms used in a conjugation.

Voice: Indicates relation of the subject of the verb to the action of the verb. There are two voices:
Active Voice: The subject is doing the action. Example: "John threw the ball."
Passive Voice: The subject is being acted upon. Example: "The ball was thrown by John."

Mood: Tells how the action or state-of-being of the verb is conceived. There are four kinds of mood.

Indicative: Expresses the action or state-of-being of the verb as a fact.
Subjunctive: Expresses that the action or state-of-being of the verb may happen or that it is doubtful that it will happen.
Conditional: Expresses that the action or state-of-being of the verb depends on something else happening first or at the same time.
Imperative: Demands that the action of the verb be carried out.

Tense: Explains at what time the action of the verb takes place or when the state-of-being occurs. There are six tenses.

Present: The action or state-of-being is now.
Past: The action or state-of-being was already.

Future: The action or state-of-being is forthcoming.
Present Perfect: Expresses that an action has been completed by the time of the speech.
Past Perfect: The speaker indicates that an action was completed by a certain point in the past.
Future Perfect: The speaker indicates that an action will be completed by a certain point in the future.

Number: Expresses whether the subject is singular or plural.

Person: Expresses who is referred to by the verb: the speaker or speakers (I, we); the one or ones spoken to (you, you); or one or more spoken about (he, she, it, they).

Form: A verb or verb phrase changes with changes in the tense and meaning. The form of the verb is the arrangement of words for any one particular meaning. There are six forms.

Simple: The basic form of a verb, without any other words necessary to express its meaning.
Emphatic: This form adds *do, did, will,* or *shall* in order to strengthen the action of the verb.
Progressive: This form expresses the action or state-of-being as in a state of continuance, that it will continue to happen or did continue to happen after the time of the speech.
Gerunds: A verb used as a noun. Example: *Walking* is fun.

Participle: A verb used as an adjective. Example: The *playing* children ran into the street.

Infinitive: A verb used as a noun, usually introduced by "to." Example: The car was unable *to stop*.

Conjugation of the Regular Verb "To Walk"

ACTIVE VOICE

Indicative Mood

Singular	Plural

PRESENT TENSE

Simple

1. I walk — we walk
2. you walk — you walk
3. he walks — they walk

Emphatic

1. I do walk — we do walk
2. you do walk — you do walk
3. he does walk — they do walk

Progressive

1. I am walking — we are walking
2. you are walking — you are walking
3. he is walking — they are walking

PAST TENSE

Simple

1. I walked — we walked
2. you walked — you walked
3. he walked — they walked

Emphatic

1. I did walk — we did walk
2. you did walk — you did walk
3. he did walk — they did walk

Singular	Plural

Progressive

1. I was walking — we were walking
2. you were walking — you were walking
3. he was walking — they were walking

FUTURE TENSE

Simple

1. I shall walk — we shall walk
2. you will walk — you will walk
3. he will walk — they will walk

Emphatic

1. I will walk — we will walk
2. you shall walk — you shall walk
3. he shall walk — they shall walk

Progressive

1. I shall be walking — we shall be walking
2. you will be walking — you will be walking
3. he will be walking — they will be walking

Singular   Plural   Singular   Plural

Progressive

PRESENT PERFECT

1. I shall have   we shall have
   been walking   been walking
2. you will have   you will have
   been walking   been walking
3. he will have   they will have
   been walking   been walking

Simple

1. I have walked   we have walked
2. you have walked you have walked
3. he has walked   they have walked

Progressive

1. I have been   we have been
   walking   walking
2. you have been   you have been
   walking   walking
3. he has been   they have been
   walking   walking

Subjunctive Mood

PRESENT TENSE

Simple

1. if I walk   if we walk
2. if you walk   if you walk
3. if he walk   if they walk

PAST PERFECT

Simple

1. I had walked   we had walked
2. you had walked you had walked
3. he had walked   they had walked

Emphatic

1. if I do walk   if we do walk
2. if you do walk   if you do walk
3. if he do walk   if they do walk

Progressive

1. I had been   we had been
   walking   walking
2. you had been   you had been
   walking   walking
3. he had been   they had been
   walking   walking

Progressive

1. if I be   if we be
   walking   walking
2. if you be   if you be
   walking   walking
3. if he be   if they be
   walking   walking

FUTURE PERFECT

Simple

1. I shall have   we shall have
   walked   walked
2. you will have   you will have
   walked   walked
3. he will have   they will have
   walked   walked

PAST TENSE

Simple

1. if I walked   if we walked
2. if you walked   if you walked
3. if he walked   if they walked

Emphatic

1. if I did walk   if we did walk
2. if you did walk   if you did walk
3. if he did walk   if they did walk

Singular	Plural

Progressive

1. if I were walking — if we were walking
2. if you were walking — if you were walking
3. if he were walking — if they were walking

PRESENT PERFECT

Simple

1. if I have walked — if we have walked
2. if you have walked — if you have walked
3. if he has walked — if they have walked

Progressive

1. if I have been walking — if we have been walking
2. if you have been walking — if you have been walking
3. if he has been walking — if they have been walking

PAST PERFECT

Simple

1. if I had walked — if we had walked
2. if you had walked — if you had walked
3. if he had walked — if they had walked

Progressive

1. if I had been walking — if we had been walking
2. if you had been walking — if you had been walking
3. if he had been walking — if they had been walking

Singular	Plural

Conditional Mood

PRESENT TENSE

Simple

1. I should walk — we should walk
2. you would walk — you would walk
3. he would walk — they would walk

Emphatic

1. I would walk — we would walk
2. you should walk — you should walk
3. he should walk — they should walk

Progressive

1. I should be walking — we should be walking
2. you would be walking — you would be walking
3. he would be walking — they would be walking

PERFECT

Simple

1. I should have walked — we should have walked
2. you would have walked — you would have walked
3. he would have walked — they would have walked

Progressive

1. I should have been walking — we should have been walking
2. you would have been walking — you would have been walking
3. he would have been walking — they would have been walking

Imperative Mood

Simple: **walk**

Emphatic: **do walk**

Progressive: **be walking**

PRESENT INFINITIVE

Simple: **to walk**

Progressive: **to be walking**

Gerund: **walking**

PERFECT INFINITIVE

Simple: **to have walked**

Progressive: **to have been walking**

Gerund: **having walked**

PARTICIPLES

Present: **walking**

Perfect Simple: **having walked**

PASSIVE VOICE

Indicative Mood

Singular   Plural

PRESENT TENSE

1. **I am walked**   **we are walked**
2. **you are walked**   **you are walked**
3. **he is walked**   **they are walked**

PAST TENSE

1. **I was walked**   **we were walked**
2. **you were walked**   **you were walked**
3. **he was walked**   **they were walked**

Singular   Plural

FUTURE TENSE

1. **I shall be walked**   **we shall be walked**
2. **you will be walked**   **you will be walked**
3. **he will be walked**   **they will be walked**

PRESENT PERFECT

1. **I have been walked**   **we have been walked**
2. **you have been walked**   **you have been walked**
3. **he has been walked**   **they have been walked**

PAST PERFECT

1. **I had been walked**   **we had been walked**
2. **you had been walked**   **you had been walked**
3. **he had been walked**   **they had been walked**

FUTURE PERFECT

1. **I shall have been walked**   **we shall have been walked**
2. **you will have been walked**   **you will have been walked**
3. **he will have been walked**   **they will have been walked**

Subjunctive Mood

PRESENT TENSE

1. **if I be walked**   **if we be walked**
2. **if you be walked**   **if you be walked**
3. **if he be walked**   **if they be walked**

Singular	Plural

PAST TENSE

1. if I were walked
2. if you were walked
3. if he were walked

if we were walked
if you were walked
if they were walked

PRESENT PERFECT

1. if I have been walked
2. if you have been walked
3. if he has been walked

if we have been walked
if you have been walked
if they have been walked

PAST PERFECT

1. if I had been walked
2. if you had been walked
3. if he had been walked

if we had been walked
if you had been walked
if they had been walked

Conditional Mood

PRESENT TENSE

1. I should be walked
2. you would be walked
3. he would be walked

we should be walked
you would be walked
they would be walked

PERFECT

1. I should have been walked
2. you would have been walked
3. he would have been walked

we should have been walked
you would have been walked
they would have been walked

Imperative Mood

Simple: to be walked

PRESENT INFINITIVE

Simple: to be walked

Gerund: being walked

PERFECT INFINITIVE

Simple: to have been walked

Gerund: having been walked

PARTICIPLES

Present: being walked

Past: walked

Perfect: having been walked

2. Using Pronouns

The pronoun is a difficult part of speech to use properly. There are many different forms of pronouns, and all of them are easy to confuse. Using pronouns correctly is also difficult because we often hear them used incorrectly. You may want to have a copy of the rules of proper pronoun usage nearby when you are writing.

Like nouns, pronouns have three forms: the Nominative Case, the Possessive Case, and the Objective Case. The meanings of the different cases are explained in this chart.

Cases of Pronouns

Nominative Case   Used for the subject or predicate nominative.

Possesive Case   Used to indicate ownership.

Objective Case   Used for the objects of prepositions and verbs.

A chart which shows the different forms of the pronoun is called a *declension*. That name came from the assumption that the Nominative Case is the primary form of a noun or pronoun. Therefore, all other cases fall away, or *decline*, from the Nominative.

Declension of the Pronoun

First Person, Masculine and Feminine
PERSONAL

	Singular	Plural
Nominative	I	we
Possessive	my, mine	our, ours
Objective	me	us

Second Person, Masculine and Feminine

Nominative	you	you
Possessive	your, yours	your, yours
Objective	you	you

Third Person, Masculine, Feminine, Neuter

Nominative	he, she, it	they
Possessive	his, her, hers, its	their, theirs
Objective	him, her, it	them

RELATIVE

	Singular	Plural
Nominative	who	who
Possessive	whose	whose
Objective	whom	whom

Rules for Using Pronouns

1. Use a singular pronoun to refer to the indefinite words *anyone, either, everyone, each, every, nobody.*

> *Everyone* has *his* own tennis racket.
> *Neither* of the girls had *her* ticket.
> *Each* of the cats has had *its* lunch.

2. Use the Nominative Case as the subject of a finite verb. (A finite verb comes at the end of the sentence and is not the main action of the sentence. Sometimes, as in the first example below, the verb doesn't even appear. The missing verb in this case is *am*.")

She is taller than *I*.

Mark is the man *who* we want to be driven home.

Give the grand prize to *whoever* comes in last.

(In the last example, *whoever* is the subject of *comes*, not the object of the preposition *to*.)

3. Use the Nominative Case after a linking verb. For examples of this, see the note on page xx.

4. Use the Possessive Case to modify a gerund. (A gerund is a verb used as a noun.)

I hated to hear *his* crying.

I heard of *their* having been lost.

5. Use the Objective Case for the object of a verb or for the object of a preposition.

Read the words to *whomever* you find.

Whom did you hear?

Martha gave the candles to Jeffrey and *me*.

Seven of *us* scouts went skiing.

3. Agreement

A writer must be careful to have the subject and verb in a sentence agree with each other in number. Here are three reminders to help you keep your subject in agreement with your verb.

1. Use a singular verb with a singular subject.
"Viki doesn't like to write." (Instead of "Viki *don't...")*

Each of us *is* buying a computer.
Neither of the heaters *is* working.
None of the pots *is* boiling.
Dan, along with the group of friends, *is* here.

2. Use a plural verb with a plural subject.

Viki and *Ralph don't* like to write.
Fertilizer and *water are* necessary for growth.
There are other fish in the sea.
Dan and *a group of friends are* here.

3. Words like *crowd, group, family,* and *committee* are called collective nouns. They may take either a singular or a plural verb according to the meaning intended.

The family is huge.
The family are enraged at the decision. (In this case, "family" means a collection of several members, each of whom is enraged.)

Punctuation

You are probably familiar with the basic rules and usage of punctuation. You know that a period often shows up at the end of a sentence. There are a few punctuation rules, however, which many writers find easy to forget. Review these rules now and then in order to keep your writing consistent.

The Colon

1. The colon is used to separate two sentences when the second explains more fully the meaning of the first.

> Dianne's typing is careless: she has twelve errors in the first sentence.

The colon may be used before a second sentence which gives the reason for the first sentence.

> Scott won't be in school tomorrow: he caught pneumonia.

2. The colon may be used before a list or to introduce a quotation.

> Many people expected a Christmas gift from me: Mom, Dad, Eleanor, Charles, Murphy, and, of course, Spot.
> The document read: "The title to your property is unclear."

The Semi-Colon

1. The semi-colon is used to separate coordinate sentences when a conjunction is not used.

> Your appearance delighted my mother; it startled me.

2. When you use the conjunctions *therefore, however, nevertheless, besides, also,* and *otherwise,* you can use a semi-colon to separate the first clause from the second. These conjunctions are stronger than those such as *and,* and they can often use a stronger break.

> Frank cut his thumb severely; therefore he was unable to finish the carving.

The Comma

1. Use a comma before a conjunction beginning an independent clause (one which contains a subject and a verb).

> It was years before he was able to return, and the city had changed a great deal in that time.

2. When recording a list of things, or when using a series of adjectives, put commas between each item or adjective. Do not put a comma after the last item or adjective.

> She brought ham, cake, sausage, and bread to the show.

3. A comma is used after an introductory phrase and encloses a parenthetical expression.

> With great respect, they lowered their heads.
> The lamp, as I have said before, is on fire.

4. A comma goes inside of the quotation mark when writing direct speech.

"Jerry is certainly crabby today," he said.

5. A comma marks off words used in addressing a person.

Carl, we'd like you to sit over there.

I would be delighted, Eileen, if you would sing for us.

The Question Mark

1. The question mark is used after a direct question but not after an indirect one.

Where is my slipper?

I asked him where my slipper is.

2. A question mark belongs inside of quotation marks if the quoted material is a question. Otherwise, it goes on the outside of the quotation mark.

"When will we see you again?" John asked.

Why did you say, "I won't do it"?

The Dash

1. The dash is used to indicate an afterthought or further explanation, or to indicate an unexpected turn in the sentence.

I noticed that my fish--you know, the brown angel—was covered with small brown spots.

There is only one thing wrong with my skating—I fall too often.

The Hyphen

1. Use a hyphen between the words of a compound adjective. Do not use a hyphen after an adverb in a compound adjective. A hyphenated compound adjective occurs only in front of the word it modifies.

The much-searched-for manuscript was finally located.
The manuscript was much searched for.
Linda gave her patient the kid-glove treatment.
The delicately balanced acrobat started wobbling.

The Apostrophe

1. Use an apostrophe to indicate the possessive case.

The girl's shoe. (singular)
The girls' team. (plural)

Writing Guidelines

Now that you understand the rules of grammar and punctuation, it is time to put them to use. This section contains a list of guidelines for clear, bold writing. They apply to every kind of writing you need to do. You can use these rules whether you are composing a business letter or a school essay or a research paper.

1. **Have something to say.** Think about your topic and understand it clearly before writing a word.

2. **Limit your scope.** Is it really necessary to write everything known about your topic? Can you choose only a small segment of it to write about? Don't ramble or write about too much in one piece of writing or your meaning will become vague.

3. **Do research.** Take the time to do fact-finding research on your topic if needed. Facts are strong and are interesting to read. Be well-informed on your topic.

4. **Outline, then tell.** Sometimes it is helpful to draw an outline before writing your letter or essay. Outlines help you get from A to B to C in a logical way. After the story is organized, tell it simply and clearly. Get to the point quickly.

5. **Be modest.** It is unwise to add personal comments to a story. In serious writing, sentences which begin, "I think..." are better left unwritten. Keep yourself in the background and let the story speak for itself. Not drawing attention to yourself is good manners whether in public or in writing.

6. **Have faith in yourself.** A reader can instantly tell if the writer is squeamish about his topic or his ability to write. Don't hedge or be apologetic when saying something. Try to put things in a positive light. Remember that most of your readers are as shy about exposing themselves as you may be. Be bold.

7. **Write in a natural style.** If you are writing a humorous essay, your own style will be more convincing than if you try to imitate Steve Martin's style. Because writing is a way to reveal yourself, there is nothing to be gained in copying the tone or method of someone else. Say what you have to say in the way that is most direct for you.

Read your finished work out loud. It should read as if you were speaking your ideas to someone. Be sure that your speaking sounds natural but not too casual.

8. **Write with nouns and verbs.** They are the strongest parts of speech. Adjectives, adverbs, and adverbial complements are frequently unnecessary.

Only a litterbug leaves them lying around a sentence. Take a look at your writing. Keep only the words that are absolutely necessary to convey the meaning.

Some people use flowery language because they want to impress people. However, a practiced reader will have much more respect for a writer whose writing is clean and direct so that it can be read quickly and understood instantly. Choose the words which have exactly the meaning you intend. Avoid fancy words and phrases.

9. **Revise and rewrite.** If you have carefully followed a good outline, usually the order of your writing is acceptable. Sometimes, seeing a finished piece of writing suggests to you that there is a better way or order in which to write it. Then you must revise your piece.

Except for some letters, almost all writing deserves and demands rewriting of some kind. Give each sentence a hard look. Where is the litter? Take it out and start over. Often entire sections need to be rewritten. This should not discourage you. Even the finest novelists reject reams of their hard work after one re-reading.

10. **Know when to stop.** Before you start writing, decide what you mean to say. Your outline provides the natural order to your message. When you have said what you intend, stop writing.

Don't waste your reader's time with an ending paragraph which only says again what you said before. However, if the form of your writing is, "Because of Event **A,** and because of Event **B,** then Event **C** happened," make Event **C** a summary paragraph. This rule helps you to avoid wordiness.

Exercises

These are exercises for developing your writing skill. They are grouped in three stages: Recognition Exercises, Style Exercises, and Writing Exercises.

Answers to these exercises begin on page 54.

Recognition Exercises

One way to criticize your own writing is to learn to recognize the parts of speech and the parts of the sentence. As you do these exercises, refer back to the discussions of the parts of speech and the parts of the sentence.

Challenge Tests: Which parts of speech do you recognize easily? Which do you need to learn better? If you get two or more wrong, return to the definitions and do further exercises.

The Noun

Write on a sheet of paper the numbers of the words in this list which are nouns.

1. narrow
2. people
3. several
4. Mexico
5. want
6. camp
7. money
8. hunger
9. music
10. windy
11. law
12. Mary
13. noisy
14. art
15. gentle
16. crowd

The Adjective

On a sheet of paper, write the number of the sentence and the adjective or adjectives it contains.

1. He had a sore foot.
2. John made an angry face.
3. The German soldier fled the dogs.
4. He climbed through the opened window.
5. I am an English pirate.
6. The spotted cat lapped the milk.
7. The average man finds taxes high.
8. The tea cup rattled in the saucer.
9. The car had a flat tire.
10. The big leaguer was unhappy with his contract.

The Verb

Write on a sheet of paper the numbers of the words in this list which are verbs.

1. under	6. think
2. jerked	7. love
3. among	8. climb
4. quietly	9. game
5. mumbled	10. polish

On your paper, write the number of the sentence, the verb of the sentence, and the tense of the verb: past, present, or future.

1. The bird flew high over the trees.
2. He is thinking about the problem.
3. He ate a peach.
4. Betty loves her pet.
5. He studied the picture carefully.
6. The boy realized his mistake.
7. She will go to the doctor tomorrow.
8. They believe in ghosts.
9. John rowed his canoe across the lake.
10. I shall hit the ball over the fence.

The Adverb

On a sheet of paper, write the number of the sentence and the adverb it contains.

1. Swiftly the jet plane crossed the sky.
2. He stood up reluctantly.
3. She ran fast.
4. He was unusually handsome.
5. He banged his fist repeatedly on the table.
6. The clerk took the money indifferently.
7. Gradually the mountains appeared in the distance.
8. She wore boots occasionally.
9. He yelled loudly for his friend.
10. They all whispered softly.

The Pronoun

On a sheet of paper, write the number of the sentence and the pronoun or pronouns it contains.

1. They ran the race.
2. Todd took it to the store.
3. Carol told me a story.
4. I loved her very much.
5. The crowd roared their approval of him.
6. The ghost frightened her.
7. We all wanted to win.
8. He called the shots.
9. Did Dad tell you the idea?
10. The prize went to them.

The Conjunction

On your sheet of paper write the number of the sentence and the conjunction or conjunctions it contains.

1. We gave them a dozen roses and a trophy.
2. You can work at home or work at school.
3. The room reflected shades of a forest: greens, browns, and yellows.
4. We could tolerate neither the laughter nor the screams.
5. Jack and Jill went up the hill.
6. I wanted to come; therefore they were willing to take me.
7. The lights of the city and the soft wind were romantic.
8. He didn't leave, although it was time to go.
9. The Jones's, the Smith's, and the Kell's are coming.
10. Eventually we will come, but not now.

The Preposition

Write the number of the sentence and the preposition or prepositions it contains.

1. I am in the house near the airport.
2. My slipper fell under the bed.
3. The boy was asleep on the haystack.
4. The book underneath the desk was John's.
5. He took the dirt road by the sawmill.
6. They heard a shout across the meadow.
7. His voice echoed back from the hills.
8. The ball bounced between first and second base.
9. The airplane flew over the desert.
10. He sat precariously above the snake.

These exercises have you use your surroundings to learn the parts of speech.

The Noun

1. A noun names persons, places, or things. Look around your room. What nouns can you see? Write down their names.
2. Bring ten objects to your table and write down their names.
3. Abstract nouns are ideas or concepts which can't be seen. How many of them can you think of?
4. Write ten names of groups of people, places, or things. These are called collective nouns.

The Adjective

1. Look outside. Choose an object and think of as many words as you can that tell about it. Write these down with the noun they modify and select the best of your choices. Watch for sloppy descriptions.
2. Find strong adjectives to modify these nouns: tree, garden, sidewalk, weather, rain, cushion, lamp, ashtray, window, mirror, furnace, book.

The Verb

1. Perform ten actions or movements while sitting on your chair, and write down what they are.
2. Abstract verbs, such as *dreaming* or *thinking*, describe a mental action or concept. How many can you think of? How many actions can you do without moving at all?
3. Write about ten of your actions using the passive voice.

The Adverb

1. Refer to the ten actions you performed for Verb Exercise 1 above. Write adverbs to modify those verbs.
2. Ask a friend to perform ten various actions. Write down the verb and an adverb describing each action.

Irregular Verbs

Refer to the section on Conjugation to refresh your memory. Then conjugate the irregular verb, "to be," on the following chart. A completed chart is on page 57.

Conjugation of the Irregular Verb "To Be"

Singular		Plural	
PRONOUN	VERB	PRONOUN	VERB
Present			
1.			
2.			
3.			
Past			
1.			
2.			
3.			
Future			
1.			
2.			
3.			

The Preposition

Perform the actions described in these sentences. Make a list of the prepositions found in the sentences.

1. Place the pencil on the floor.
2. Put the pen and pencil in a box.
3. Place the ruler under the chair.
4. Put the pen between the ruler and the pencil.
5. Place the eraser in the pencil case with the ruler.
6. Push the chair against the table.

The Interjection

1. Think of ten different interjections which could begin a sentence.
2. Think of three different interjections that are not usually interjections (such as, "Hello!").

Style Exercises

1. Answer the following questions when reviewing your writing:

A) Do you find more active voice or passive voice verbs?
B) Do you find more adjectives than nouns?
C) Do you find more adverbs than verbs?

Ask these questions of the writing of your favorite authors. Compare their writing patterns with your own.

2. Rewrite this paragraph by E. B. White on a sheet of paper. It will be used to teach you to analyze your own style and the style of other writers. You will learn whether you are using active voice verbs, careful nouns, and well-chosen adjectives and adverbs. You can check to see if you are using too many adverbial complements.

Suddenly Stuart opened his eyes and sat up. He thought about the letter he had sent and he wondered whether it had ever been delivered. It was an unusually small letter, of course, and might have gone unnoticed in a letter box. This idea filled him with fears and worries. But soon he let his thoughts return to the river, and as he lay there a whippoorwill began to sing on the opposite shore, darkness spread over the land, and Stuart dropped off to sleep.

You will need an assortment of colored pencils for this exercise. Using the following key, initial above each word its part of speech.

black **n** = noun
blue **adj** = adjective
brown **pro** = pronoun
purple **va** = verb (active voice)
red **vp** = verb (passive voice)
orange **adv** = adverb
pink **c** = conjunction
green **prep** = preposition
yellow **i** = interjection

After you have initialed all the words in this paragraph, identify the parts of the sentence using this key:
- circle the predicates in red
- underline the subjects once in black
- underline the direct objects once in black and once in red
- underline the indirect objects three times in black
- draw an orange jagged line under the adverbial complements
- draw a blue curvy line under the attributives

After you have done this, study your work for a few minutes. Look closely at the color patterns. Then answer these questions:

1. Do you find many direct objects (indicating active voice verbs)?

2. Do you find many sentences with adverbial complements? Count the number of simple sentences versus the number of complex sentences (those with adverbial complements). Do you have many of both?

3. What can you say about E. B. White's style? Does he use frequent passive voice verbs, adjectives, adverbs, or adverbial complements. Is his meaning always clear?

4. Take a piece of your own writing. It could be a letter, a story, or a short summary of a TV show or movie. Use Style Exercise 2 on your own writing. Ask the same questions. How can you improve your style? Where are your weaknesses?

Writing Exercises

You won't write well if you don't write. Here are some ideas to start you writing and to keep you writing.

1. Get a tablet and a folder. You should write on **looseleaf paper which you can rip out**. Bound journals can be intimidating, as the writing seems to be so permanent. After you write, place finished pieces in your folder and date them. Compare your progress.

2. Think of something important to you and explain it to your reader. If ideas come to you about topics you know well, write them down. The best writing is always done by someone who completely understands the subject.

3. Summarize experiences: movies, plays, trips, conversations, or articles you read. Trips to art galleries can be excellent sources of thought and inspiration. Perhaps sports or spectator games interest you. If you know something, write it down.

4. Periodically test your writing:
   A) Use the Writing Guidelines of this book.
   B) Use the Style Exercises to spot check your clumsy sentences.
   C) Compare your latest writing to your older pieces. Are you improving? Are you sneaking back to excess adverbs?

5. *Sentence Repairing*   Test the following sentences first by reading them out loud. Do they sound awkward? If they do, rewrite them using this key for repairing sentences.

Sentence Repairing Key

A. Certain adverbs are awkward and unnecessary, such as *the fact that, owing to, in spite of, call your attention to.* Others are more easily expressed as adjectives.

B. Frequently, attributives such as *who is* and *which is* are unnecessary.

C. An active voice verb is stronger than a passive voice verb, although it is not usable all of the time.

D. Adverbial complements should be placed next to the words they modify.

1. Accusedly talking, she called the attention of the driver to the dent in her fender.

2. The dog which was an extremely large one lived down by the railroad tracks.

3. We were awed by the bountifully scrumptious Thanksgiving dinner.

4. Owing to the extremely gracious manner of the girl who lived in the house, we felt welcome.

5. Father, who is near the age of retirement, plans to build a cabin which would be made of logs.

6. He is a very courageously acting man who is able to face danger.

7. A soldier was dancing with a sprained ankle.

8. A theme paper was written of amazing length by a young man who was long-winded.

9. The fact that she sews well makes all the members of the family come to her who is an excellent seamstress to sew their buttons on.

10. Here in the living room is the piano which owing to the fact that my grandfather gave it to my mother, I own.

When used properly, adverbial complements give variety to good writing. Rewrite and reorganize these simple sentences into a varied and interesting paragraph:

We were preparing for a trip. Dad forgot to set the alarm. We were running late. The temperature was five below zero. Our hot water pipes were frozen. We had to thaw them with electric wire tape. The house wouldn't get warmer. Our furnace wouldn't start. We were nearly frantic. We confusedly tried to wash up and dress in the bitter cold. We carried five suitcases down to the garage. We packed them in the trunk. We all climbed into the car, grumpy and cold. But we just sat. The garage door was frozen shut.

Answers to Recognition Exercises
Page 40

The Noun: 2, 4, 6, 7, 8, 9, 11, 12, 14, 16

The Adjective:

1. sore
2. angry
3. German
4. opened
5. English

6. spotted
7. average, high
8. tea
9. flat
10. big, unhappy

The Verb: 2, 5, 6, 7, 8, 10

1. flew (past)
2. is thinking (present)
3. ate (past)
4. loves (present)
5. studied (past)

6. realized (past)
7. will go (future)
8. believe (present)
9. rowed (past)
10. shall hit (future)

The Adverb:

1. Swiftly
2. reluctantly
3. fast
4. usually
5. repeatedly

6. indifferently
7. Gradually
8. occasionally
9. loudly
10. softly

The Pronoun:

1. They
2. it
3. me
4. I, her
5. him

6. her
7. We
8. He
9. you
10. them

The Conjunction:

1. and
2. or
3. and
4. neither, nor
5. and

6. therefore
7. and
8. although
9. over
10. but

The Preposition:

1. in
2. under
3. on
4. underneath
5. by

6. across
7. from
8. between
9. over
10. above

Possible Answers to Recognition Exercises

Page 44

The Noun:

1. chair, table, wall, floor, window, rug, pencil, desk, plant, curtains
2. pen, eraser, pencil, plant, book, paper, newspaper, picture, pin, vase
3. love, hope, charity, faith, law, order, trust, anger, happiness, joy, peace
4. herd, flock, bunch, gang, crowd

The Adjective:

1. cloud: grayish, fluffy, large, low, misty, cumulus, whitish (*grayish* and *whitish* are sloppy)

2. majestic tree   soft cushion
   bountiful garden   squat lamp
   cracked sidewalk   dirty ashtray
   stormy weather   sparkling window
   misty rain   huge mirror
   rumbling furnace   exciting book

The Verb:

1. snap, stamp, talk, look, see, shout, move, smile, laugh, frown
2. love, plan, hope, excite, trust, dream, think, wish, plot, remember, regret
3. I was loved. My day is planned. The trip was hoped for. The dog is excited by the bone. My friend was trusted.

The Adverb:

1. snap harshly; stamp firmly; talk incessantly; look wistfully; see clearly; shout loudly; move slowly; smile sweetly; laugh softly; frown darkly
2. tie slowly; look intently; speak softly; work quickly; smile brightly; place carefully; write neatly; write quickly; turn slowly; sit quietly

Irregular Verbs:

Singular		Plural	
PRONOUN	**VERB**	**PRONOUN**	**VERB**
Present			
1. I	am	we	are
2. you	are	you	are
3. he, she it	is	they	are
Past			
1. I	was	we	were
2. you	were	you	were
3. he, she, it	was	they	were
Future			
1. I	will be	we	will be
2. you	will be	you	will be
3. he, she, it	will be	they	will be

The Preposition:

1. on
2. in
3. under
4. between
5. in, with
6. against

The Interjection:

1. Oh!, Alas!, Goodness!, Hi!, Ouch!, Bye!, Bang!, Wham!, Yea!
2. Goodbye!, Wait!, Roger! (or any other name used as an interjection)

Style Exercises
Page 48

       adv.   n.   va. adj n.   c va. adv.

Suddenly Stuart opened his eyes and sat up.

pro.   va   adj n pro.   va. c pro.

He thought about the letter he had sent and he

  va   c   pro. va adv   va

wondered whether it had ever been delivered.

pro va adj   adv   adj   n   prep n   c

It was an unusually small letter, of course, and

    va   adj   prep adj   n   adj

might have gone unnoticed in a letter box. This

  n   va   pro prep n   c   n   c

idea filled him with fears and worries. But

adv pro va adv. n.   va prep adj n   c

soon he let his thoughts return to the river, and

prep pro va adv adj   n   va   n   prep

as he lay there a whippoorwill began to sing on

adj   adj   n   n   va   prep adj

the opposite shore, darkness spread over the

  n   c   n   va   adv   n

land, and Stuart dropped off to sleep.

Possible Answers to Writing Exercises
Page 51

5.

1. She accused the driver of denting her fender.
2. The large dog lived down by the railroad tracks.
3. Thanksgiving dinner awed us.
4. Since the girl was gracious, we felt welcome in her home.
5. When Father retires, he plans to build a log cabin.
6. He is a courageous man able to face danger.
7. A soldier with a sprained ankle was dancing.
8. A long-winded young man wrote a long term paper.
9. Since she is an excellent seamstress, all the members of the family ask her to sew their buttons.
10. My mother gave me the piano in the living room which my grandfather gave her.

One very cold morning, we were preparing for a trip. Because Dad forgot to set the alarm, we were running late. First we discovered our hot water pipes were frozen, so we had to thaw them out with electric wire tape. Then we noticed that the house wasn't getting warmer. Somehow our furnace hadn't started. Frantic and confused, we tried to wash and dress in the bitter cold. We carried five suitcases down to the garage and packed them into the trunk. Grumpy and cold, we climbed into the car, only to sit: for our garage door was frozen shut.